To: Alexander

From: Grandma & Grandpa

Date: March 11, 2011
5th Birthday

A Special Fish for Jonah

Because God Has a Job for Everyone

Written and Illustrated by
Andy McGuire

HARVEST HOUSE PUBLISHERS

EUGENE, OREGON

For my Daughter, Jane,
a very special fish in her own right.

A SPECIAL FISH FOR JONAH
Copyright © 2010 by Andy McGuire

Published by Harvest House Publishers
Eugene, OR 97402
www.harvesthousepublishers.com

ISBN: 978-0-7369-2561-7

Artwork © Andy McGuire and published in association with the Books & Such Literary Agency,
52 Mission Circle, Suite 122, PMB 170, Santa Rosa, CA 95409-5370, www.booksandsuch.biz

Design and production by Franke Design and Illustration, Minneapolis, Minnesota

Printed in Singapore

10 11 12 13 14 15 /IM/ 10 9 8 7 6 5 4 3 2 1

BEFORE WE BEGIN...

God told Jonah to go to a city called Ninevah, but Jonah didn't like the people who lived there. So he hopped on a boat going the other way. While he was sailing, God stirred up such a terrible storm that the people on the boat had to throw Jonah into the sea to save themselves. But what happened to Jonah? God prepared a special fish to swallow him whole and then spit him out on land, on his way to Ninevah.

How did God pick the special fish? Maybe, just maybe,
He asked an angelfish to look into it.

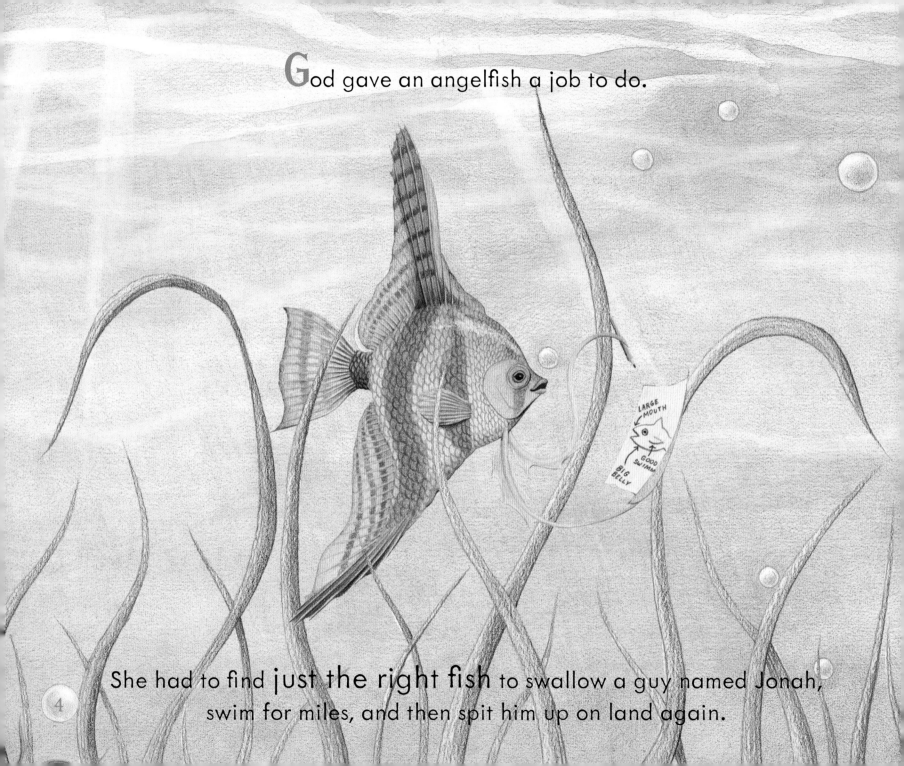

God gave an angelfish a job to do.

She had to find just the right fish to swallow a guy named Jonah, swim for miles, and then spit him up on land again.

4

A lot of fish were interested in the job,
but she couldn't take just any fish.

Too small.

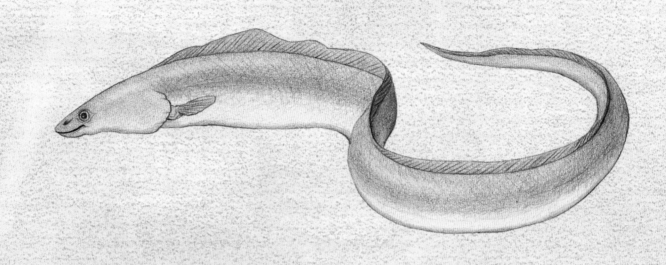

Too skinny.

Too **FLAT.**

Too SCARY.

Too hungry.

You're really more of a **sinker** than a swimmer.

That's **cheating!**

Nice *try*, but I don't think so.

The angelfish interviewed hundreds of fish, but she just

CARP FISH OCTOPUS TUNA SALMON SNAPPER WALLEYE WALRUS DIESEL-EEL ELECTRIC EEL GIANT SQUID PIRANHA HIPPO HERRING

couldn't find the right one for the job.

TRYOUT
LIST

GUPPY
GOLDFISH
CATFISH
SWORDFISH
HAMMERHEAD
GREAT WHITE
NEMO
MARLIN
HAMMER
TETRA
BASS
TROUT
CLAM
DOLPHIN
BELUGA
HUMPBACK
STING RAY
MANTA RAY

17

But just as the angelfish **was about** to give up and go back to the reef, she saw a big, **funny-looking fish** hanging out **all alone** in a corner of the ocean floor.

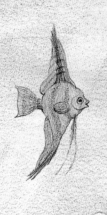

"**H**ey! What kind of fish are you?" the angelfish asked.
"I'm **Specialfish**," the big fish answered.
"What's a special fish?" she asked.

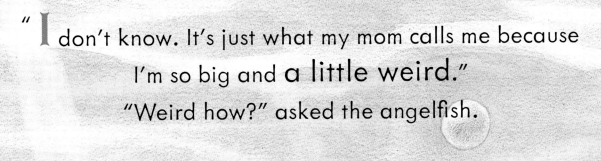

"I don't know. It's just what my mom calls me because I'm so big and **a little weird.**"

"Weird how?" asked the angelfish.

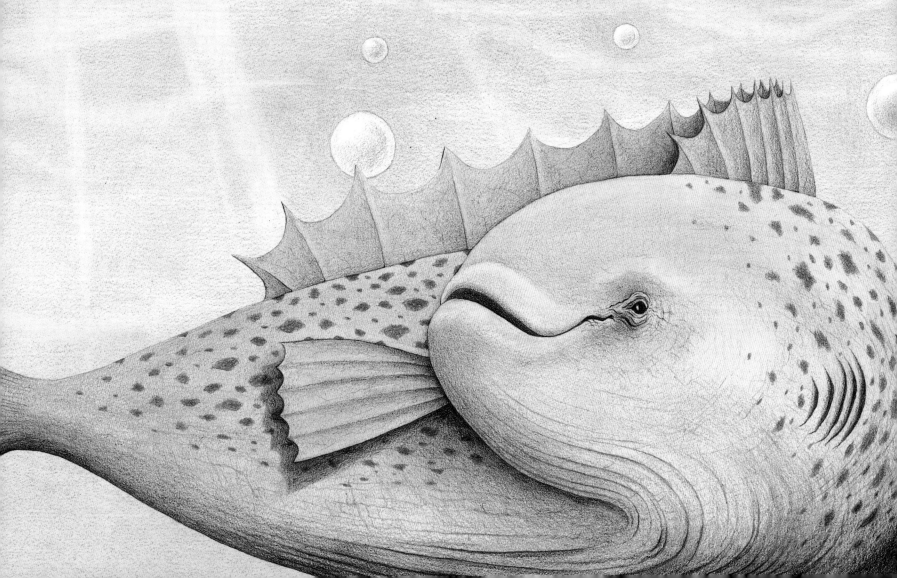

Suddenly Specialfish saw an anchor drop beside him and in a moment he **swallowed it whole.**

"That **was** weird," said the angelfish.

"I'll swallow **anything**," said Specialfish.
"I've swallowed furniture and tools and toys
and treasure chests and small boats.
If it falls in the water, I'll **swallow** it."

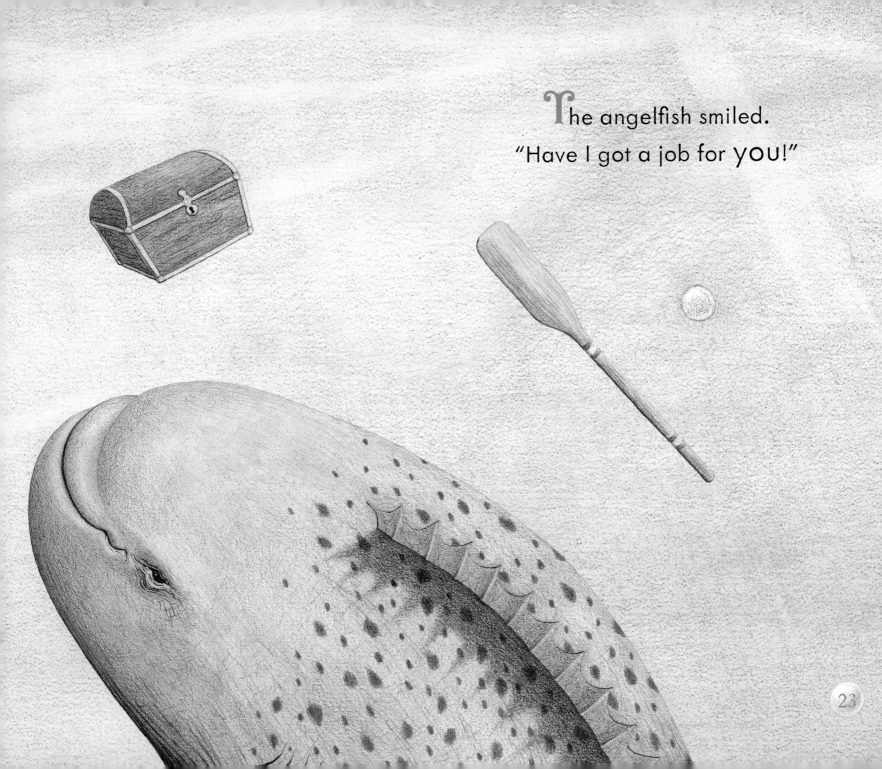

The angelfish smiled.
"Have I got a job for YOU!"

The angelfish took Specialfish to the boat God had told them about, and they **waited for the storm.** Many other fish came to watch.

GO SPECIALFISH

YOU

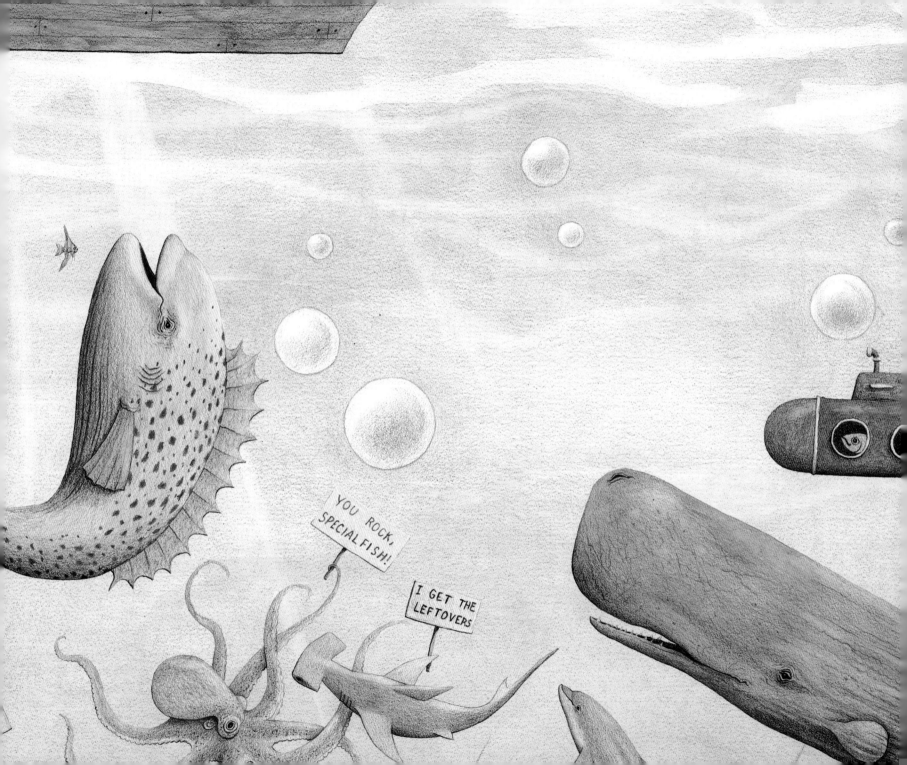

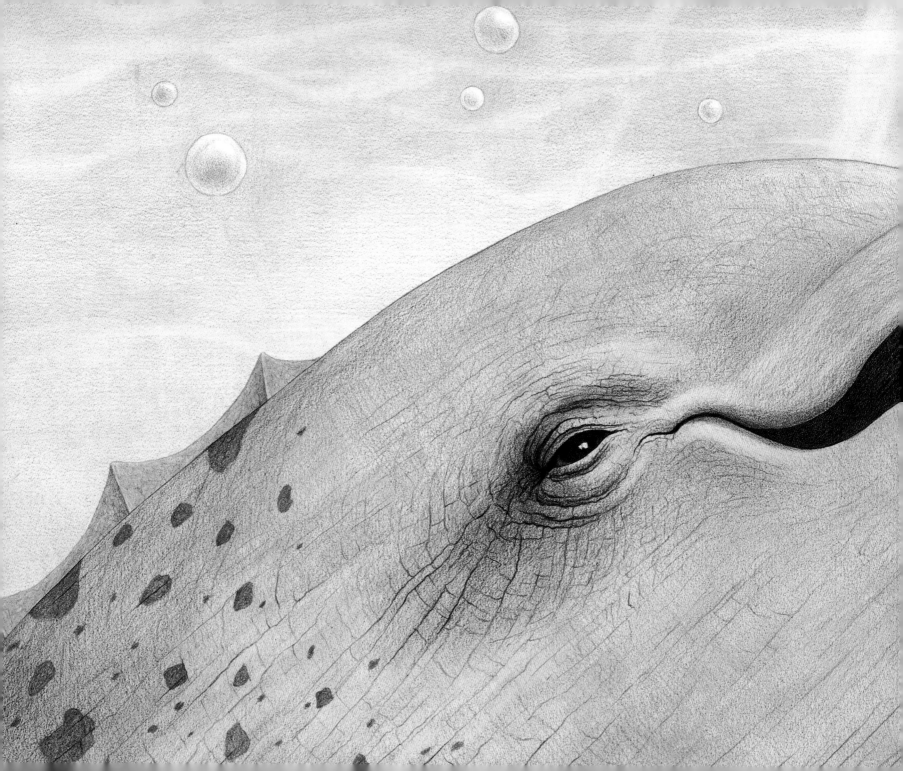

Finally, the moment came and
Specialfish was **ready**.

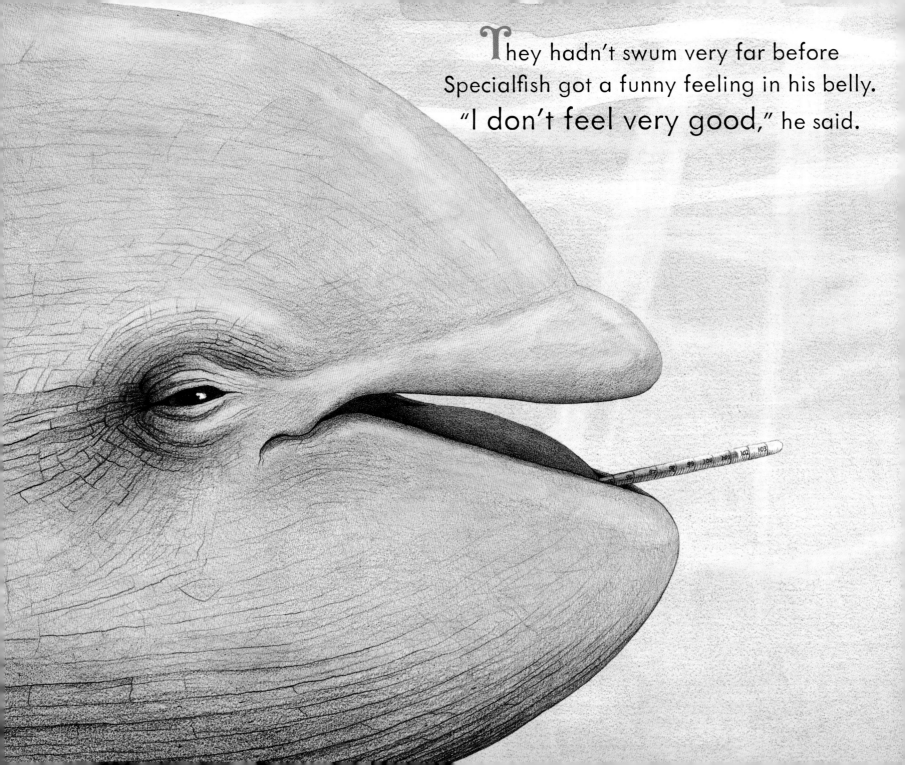

They hadn't swum very far before
Specialfish got a funny feeling in his belly.
"I don't feel very good," he said.

The angelfish smiled. "Perfect!"

As soon as they got near a beach, Specialfish spat the man out of his belly. He felt better right away. They were both pleased with a job well done.

"So what will the man do now?" asked Specialfish as they swam away. The angelfish shrugged her fins. "Who knows? Maybe God has special plans for people too."

GLOSSARY

Fin Whale

Angelfish

Blue Marlin

Beluga

Longnose Gar

Goldfish

Pinecone Fish

Tiger Shark

Manta Ray

Aba

Humpback Whale

Hammerhead Shark

Reef Shark

I ♥ PEOPLE

Giant Clam

Manatee

Red Devil Anglerfish

Octopus

Sperm Whale

Bottlenose Dolphin